Letters to Herostratus
A Collection of Short Poetry
Katarina Kelley

Queen Anne's Lace Publishing

Copyright © 2024 Queen Anne's Lace Publishing and Katarina Kelley

All rights reserved.

No portion of this book may be reproduced in any form without written permission from the publisher or author, except as permitted by U.S. copyright law.

Contents

	Dedication	VII
1.	TEMPLE	1
2.	I	3
3.	II	4
4.	III	5
5.	IV	6
6.	V	7
7.	VI	8
8.	VII	9
9.	VIII	10
10.	IX	11
11.	X	12
12.	XI	13
13.	XII	14
14.	XIII	15
15.	XIV	16

16.	XV	17
17.	XVI	18
18.	XVII	19
19.	XVIII	20
20.	XIX	21
21.	XX	22
22.	XXI	23
23.	XXII	24
24.	XXIII	25
25.	XXIV	26
26.	XXV	27
27.	XXVI	28
28.	XXVII	29
29.	XXVIII	30
30.	XXIX	31
31.	XXX	32
32.	XXXI	33
33.	XXXII	34
34.	XXXIII	35
35.	XXXIV	36
36.	XXXV	37
37.	XXXVI	38

38.	XXXVII	39
39.	XXXVIII	40
40.	XXXIX	41
41.	XL	42
42.	XLI	43
43.	XLII	44
44.	XLIII	45
45.	XLIV	46
46.	XLV	47
47.	XLVI	48
48.	XLVII	49
49.	XLVIII	50
50.	XLIX	51
51.	L	52
52.	LI	53
53.	LII	54
54.	LIII	55
55.	LIV	56
56.	LV	57
57.	LVI	58
58.	LVII	59
59.	LVIII	60

60.	FLAMES	61
61.	LIX	62
62.	LX	63
63.	LXI	64
64.	ASHES	65
65.	LXII	66
66.	LXIII	67
67.	LXIV	68
68.	LXV	69
69.	LXVI	70
70.	LXVII	71
71.	LXVIII	72
72.	LXIX	73
73.	LXX	74
74.	LXXI	75
75.	LXXII	76
76.	LXXIII	77
77.	last love letter	78
	Thank You	79
	About the author	80

Dedication

It's been a while, I still think about you every single day, stranger. This all started for you, all these beautiful words I could never so much as think of for anyone else, I even find myself having to apologize to God for taking more time to praise you than I do him. Though I can't imagine he'd be too upset if he knows you.

I heard an old folk tale some years back that if one can't sleep it's because another is dreaming about them. It may not be true but it does put a smile on my face during these long sleepless nights when I think there's a chance I might have slipped through your dreams. I'd never sleep again in all my life if I knew you would dream of me for only a minute.

I take that idea with me sometimes and think whatever hardships I go through are for you. All the endless wandering so you could have a home, my bones ache so you could rest, my very blood and sweat watering the grass so you won't have to walk in dirt.

I have no right to ask you to sully yourself with lies, but if you ever tell one, please tell me that's the truth.

I keep finding new ways to say it and I'll never run out of them, but I will save you the reading and the world some paper. I miss you.

KATARINA KELLEY

TEMPLE

I

The image of ~~Herostratus~~ couldn't possibly compare to his animation

Just to know something so good breathes in this world

Witnessing creation with the rest of us

Drown me in the depths of your simple perfection

II

The hymns I loyally sing for you make me forget the sounds of the older serenades

I stop and listen to that ancient happy melody I could still dance to

What a much sweeter way to say I miss you

III

Pain of the absence of you leaves me numb to the feeling of anything else

Pain that you'll never know

Please come back to me soon, my ~~Caesar~~, my ~~Mark Antony~~

Somehow the sun still shines and the birds still sing

Don't they know what I do? Does my misery spread to them?

IV

Chances are I wont see you tomorrow and that idea is beyond agony

Whatever comes know that I love you and I'd love for you to think of me sometimes

The only anguish worse than your absence would be your indifference

But what are the chances of the most amazing thing looking my way

V

Sometimes I try and make believe I don't miss you

I pretend it doesn't hurt, to not have you with me

As childish and selfish as it sounds, please don't be with anyone else

VI

The thought of seeing you again gives me the peace I need

That day when everything in the world is back in its place

Know that I love you more than anything, more than I should

Think of me, even if it's just once, but think of me

VII

I miss you

Your voice

Your arms

Everything about you that I fell in love with.

Don't stay away for too long ~~Darling~~

VIII

Where do I go in a world always without you?

I find myself begging my memories for the faintest trace of you

Even my dreams fail to bring me your shadow

My love, please don't leave me like this

IX

I have loved you far too long and far too deeply just to beg with words you'll never hear

Don't let me love you in vain

Come back to me ~~Darling,~~ and come back to stay

X

What a curse it is to be in love

To search the horizon for your silhouette, and the spiteful seed of hope it's you there

To search the same way through the fog of my dreams and my waking imagination

To be haunted with all the things I should have said while we were alone together

What a curse it is to be in love.

XI

Oh to abandon all lies and pretense and become only the woman seen from your eyes

It was never my intention to devolve to this, I would have loved to be something that made you happy

I am beyond the simplicity of pain and have nothing left but a great numb chasm in your absence, I seem to gain more of it every day

I've been missing your touch, your voice and your soul next to mine for far too long

XII

Is it a joy or a curse to break out of the numbness?

After a year without you my empty heart began to beat, and my cold skin began to feel

Even when I'm free your memory lingers like a phantom limb no matter how hard I try to lose it

XIII

When I think of you all I see are these pages

XIV

It took all the courage in my body to walk up to you and say goodbye for the first time

I would have ran away but you turned and took me in your arms

Though I didn't know to call it 'love' at the time I knew I would have died for you then

And I live for you now

XV

My mind wanders to the pavilion that sheltered so much of our time together

Days spent watching whatever flights of fancy distracted you for the moment

Simple pleasures that showed me our future and the children who would come to share it

XVI

That one perfect day, I'd wish for a thousand more like it, and kill for just one of the day that should have never ended

Hopeless and seemingly abandoned you came at the last minute like the heroes of old to return my heart back to my chest

Even the trees were celebrating your arrival, and the autumn sun shined rose and gold just for us

We'll have more perfect days like that, and we'll have them until we're old

Until then, ~~Mo Ghile Mear~~

XVII

I want to know what it's like to fall in love with someone who loves you back

Fall in love with me ~~Darling~~, let's find out what love is like Together

XVIII

Through the uncertainty of the endless night my equally endless love endures

My faith in us is built on that perseverance that reminds me you are and always will be

My ~~Herostratus~~

XIX

The things I cling to in failed repeated attempts at definition

Even the patch of earth where our love sprouted means nothing

It was my blood that watered it and in my heart that it's roots took hold

The only thing that ever gave me life, without you I wither and drain

XX

A rebellious child of an infinitely merciful God hardly whispering praise to the one who died for her

I don't deserve the breath in my lungs yet I have the audacity to ask for a miracle

The privilege to love my ~~Herostratus~~ like I was first loved

In the dirt or in a golden palace, what an honor that would be

XXI

Now you come to me

Not as a sweet memory, but as guilt

For years I loved you, years grasping desperately at whatever traces of your presence I could

The very moment I took my attention elsewhere your ghost pounces

I do miss when it wasn't like this

At one point I didn't have to rummage through the years without you for scraps of warmth

Once you were more than Just a statue of ~~Caesar~~

XXII

Sometimes there really is no going back

My clothes from back then have worn out, I don't remember the steps we danced together

In the unstoppable torrent of time I promise you this

I will never allow you to become a thing of the past

XXIII

Finally

After more waiting and more hoping than I knew possible

You're here

Life, love and a sleepless smiling night knowing it's the last without you

Let this be it

Let this be real

XXIV

The year between us hasn't stopped me from loving you, it only trained me to miss you

Even if creation in its entirety meant to tear us apart I would fight against it

The sickening things I do to fight the misery now I could only live with knowing you fought it too

XXV

In spite of it all we made it this far, as if anything could ever hope of stopping us.

XXVI

Two weeks now

Both a million miles and an fingertips length away

All I want is for you to wait another two weeks and promise we'll never have to wait again

I never want to wait again

XXVII

The terror of it

My best laid plans of grand romance crumbling in the most unregal manner

The very source of all my bravery plaguing me with doubt

The sudden change of yesterday's excitement to today's horror

Though my realest fear is that I'll always be here

Waiting, shaking

XXVIII

I forgot the human that I held once

How could I forget?

After all this time how could I remember?

Be the king I made you to be in my lonely dreams

XXIX

Scrambled words of scrambled love

Every night I pour them into the void I pretend is you

I wish you hadn't left me so far away from you

I wish it was easier for me to give up on you

XXX

Obsession or not, the proof of my love is in my rotting spirit

A terror and cautionary tale until the tragedy turns to comedy

Life returns and the wait is over

XXXI

What if everything was right for once?

That shouldn't be too much to ask

I'll see you tomorrow ~~Mo Ghile Mear~~

XXXII

I'm not made of gold, you were never eight feet tall

My only crown was your desire, your only throne my heart

Our kingdom built in your hand holding mine

XXXIII

Love was supposed to be a warm summer night, your hand in mine for a just moment

No

It's cold waiting, reaching for memories until death and thereafter

But for only you

I'll always be gladly waiting in the thereafter

XXXIV

Amazing reality of when these memories were the present

Endless joy of knowing they're with you too

Pleasure I could never tell you the whole of

Peace knowing you'll come back soon

XXXV

I waited years for you

Then waited more

Don't make me wait again

Because I will

XXXVI

Not one thing in this world is as it should be

I am powerless to fix any of it

If I could put one thing back in its place

I would bring you home

XXXVII

From only you

Joy you could never know

And greater peace still

In returning the smallest portion

XXXVIII

You deserve so much more than words

The mountains I should be moving, gifts I should lay at your feet

I swear to put every one of these words to action one day

XXXIX

Oh my ~~Herostratus~~

Trapped in this temporary world filled with temporary things

I promise to love you with every eternal part of me

There is no Heaven without you, ~~Mo Ghile Mear~~

XL

Bless the rain that drove me under your tent

I pray for the same divine direction towards you now

I am completely and pitifully yours as much as I am the Lord's

XLI

In the midst of the unthinkable I still reach for you

My suffering causes me to wish only the best for you

XLII

What is beyond our reach is not beyond my prayers

One day we won't be beyond either

I promise

I promise

One day

XLIII

The courage of warriors and the strength of armies

More needed still just to ask you for a dance

For you alone that courage is always within me

XLIV

Here I survive, alone in a loveless land

Foolishly finding my purpose in you

While you deserve more than any love I could give you

My heart is always yours, whether you take it or not.

XLV

I think of the home we'll share

The nights we'll spend together

Love like I only find in my dreams

And the prayers of thanks I'll send up when everything is as it should be

XLVI

I'll never have to wonder where my home or love lies

Only you in the September rain

Only where I can hear your heartbeat

XLVII

We were children once, playing and whispering together

Such a long time ago

I loved you then and I love you now

XLVIII

I would give anything to do nothing with you

And make the world small enough to fit both of us in

XLIX

If I could never feel your arms around me

Or hear the depth of your voice

I pray the memory of them never leave me

L

There is an indescribable void that still echos with music you made when we were together

I never expected you but I always wanted you, and will continue to want until my dying day

Whoever may steal my heart away from you will have to tolerate your place in it

LI

The many places I've wandered to but never belonged

I'm so homesick here, farther away from you than I've ever been

LII

I may never write down all I wanted to say to you

I thought I could live without you at first, when you were fresh in my heart and mind

Now I live my whole life with my heart in your hands, praying you'll notice and be careful

LIII

All my insignificant dreams

To pack your lunch

To sing our children to sleep

How empty my life has become without those dreams

LIV

What I wouldn't give to be twelve and in love with you again

Nothing from that time has survived this cycle of pain and grief

I've been away from my love longer than I ever have

I wait like I always have

I love like I always have

LV

Waiting for just the ghost of you is killing me

I wait in a loveless land while the dogs rip everything I am to shreds

I'm so tired of waiting thousands of years for you alone and angry

There's not much of me left waiting

LVI

I was always so afraid of the merciless flow of time

But not if I knew you were at the end of it

With something that was warm and real and mine

I have nothing to be afraid of

LVII

It's been longer than I ever could have imagined since I last saw you

I've found more than waiting in my life, and I am sorry for that

This world has taken everything from me and it may take you as well

Know that wherever I go I will always love you, even when I'm in no position to

LVIII

Even when I don't blush or kick my heels when I think of you

I don't make a single decision for the future without planning on sharing it with you

I know I'll see you again, tomorrow night or when the Lord calls us home

When we meet I can run into your arms, and let this rage and grief fall off my shoulders

And hear the voice that narrates my every dream welcome me home

FLAMES

LIX

What a temple I built around you

When we were together all of creation would fall into place around us

Surely the man with the authority to bring nature to its knees had divine purpose

But you were never the ~~Caesar~~ I knew you to be

I hardly even knew ~~Herostratus~~

And I built my home around a stranger

LX

After all these miserable years I could never discern what you were exactly

The cold unfeeling star in the distance I was never even worthy of knowing

Or the simplest of men that was only worthy by my love

The only thing I've come to know is I tore myself to shreds, without even your slightest command

LXI

So here it ends

With me leaving, heart intact

Or you coming back to finish what you started

If you never come back, as much as it pains me to write those words

By God I will live, I will dance

I learned too late that there is life without you

Though I'll never go a day without thinking of you, or a moment without loving you

This is goodbye, now or forever.

ASHES

LXII

I even miss the waiting now

The pain that kept you a part of me

And the numbness you left behind

When will that be taken from me as well?

LXIII

I would have peeled my skin off just to remember the way you touched it

This violence was never meant for anyone else

To impose my will to care for you and keep what you left me in such a manner

It could never be anyone else

LXIV

If I only knew how you would burn me

How my ashes would still long for your warmth long after

Would I have ever built this temple?

LXV

Never would I ever wish this living death for you

You will live a long life

Surrounded by people who will never love you like once I did

And in a hundred years on your last night

Let my memory creep around your neck and smother you to sleep

Whisper my name with your last breath

LXVI

It was never flames

That would be too warm for what you were

You never consumed me

I was starved

I can't feed this flame

Or douse it with water

Those aren't scars on my face

They're wrinkles

LXVII

I loved you even while I was burning

LXVIII

She had your eyes

Blue like the stars

Like you she only met me in dreams

I can't even say I lost her

LXIX

Oh how easily the tears flow now

I could hardly cry a drop while I waited

What a pathetic freedom

LXX

Moonlight still shines through memory of the night we danced

She was so proud of me on that warm summer night

What does she think of me now?

LXXI

All those great lovers who came before us

They died together and lived forever

We could have written ourselves into the very stars

And here our ashes blow away in the wind

LXXII

The empty pedestals

They all needed to burn

What I had left of you was never truly you

My ashes are as hollow as your temple ever was

LXXIII

It hurts to remember how much I loved you

How much I still love the man I thought you were

LAST LOVE LETTER

If it was only ever words between us

I am forever satisfied with just that much

In those brief moments we built Rome

Likewise our time together is an eternal thought in the mind of God

The very harmony for which the symphony of creation was first conducted

Thank You

I am so fortunate to have the support and love of friends and family while I pursue my dreams.

A special thanks to my best friend and publisher who this would not be possible without.

Also to the one holding this book who took the time out of their day to go on this journey with me, thank you.

About the Author

After writing romance fiction and love letters all through high school, Katarina Kelley compiles many of her writings in her debut "Letters to Herostratus". Katarina has always believed in turning both joy and heartbreak into art, taking inspiration from many great poets before her time, namely Dante and Virgil, she decided to try her own hand at poetry. She hopes that this will only be the beginning of a lifelong passion that she is excited to share with the world and that her work will continue to inspire others long after her time

www.ingramcontent.com/pod-product-compliance
Lightning Source LLC
Chambersburg PA
CBHW042027050526
44107CB00103B/727